D1442978

ON THE TRAIL MADE OF DAWN

ON THE TRAIL MADE OF DAWN

NATIVE AMERICAN CREATION STORIES

RETOLD BY

M. L. WEBSTER

LINNET BOOKS

North Haven, Connecticut

First published 2001 as a Linnet Book,
an imprint of The Shoe String Press, Inc.,
2 Linsley Street, North Haven, Connecticut 06473.
www.shoestringpress.com

Library of Congress Cataloging-in-Publication Data

Webster, M. L. [n. d.]
On the trail made of dawn : Native American creation stories / retold by
M.L. Webster.
    p. cm.
Includes bibliographical references.
Summary: Presents thirteen creation stories from Native American tribes,
putting them in the context of the culture and beliefs of the tribes.
ISBN 0-208-02497-2 (alk. paper)
    1. Indian mythology—North America—Juvenile literature. [1. Creation—
Folklore. 2. Indians of North America—Folklore. 3. Folklore—North
America.] I. Title.

E98.R3 W44 2001
398.2'089'97—dc21

2001029841

The paper in this publication meets the
minimum requirements of American National
Standard for Information Sciences—Permanence
of Paper for Printed Library Materials,
ANSI-Z39.48-1984. ∞

Designed by Carol Sawyer of Rose Design

Printed in the United States of America

To my children and my grandchildren with love.
To the playmates of my youth on the Ojibway Reservation
in northern Minnesota with fond memories.

❖◦❖◦❖◦❖◦❖◦❖◦❖◦❖◦❖◦❖◦❖◦❖◦❖◦❖◦◦

In the house made of dawn,
In the story made of dawn,
On the trail made of dawn,
Came the people.

—Navajo

❖◦❖◦❖◦❖◦❖◦❖◦❖◦❖◦❖◦❖◦❖◦◦

CONTENTS

AUTHOR'S NOTE

Long before the days of recorded time, the first peoples in the Americas expressed their understanding of the world through oral myths and legends. These legends tell us much about these early peoples: of their belief in powerful spirits, the creation of the earth and of the heavens above, and of the birth of human-kind and other creatures.

Generation after generation, families gathered around their fires to hear the tribal elders relate the ancient stories. Some of their spirits, heroes, and deities—such as Raven, Coyote, and Old-Man-Winter—were common to many tribes. While their tales may have varied among tribes or even among clans, the substance was the same: It is how they viewed themselves and the world around them.

Although I am not a professional storyteller, my younger days were spent sitting by a lake on warm summer evenings in northern Minnesota, listening to the legends and myths as told by elders of the Ojibway tribe. This gave me a deep appreciation of Native American culture and heritage, which I hope to foster in others with this book.

In these stories I have retold tales from thirteen different Native peoples, to introduce young children to the magic of Native American mythology and its understanding of and resonance with the natural world. These stories can be read aloud to children, and even acted out by them. They are based on older texts and, as much as possible, material originally collected orally from the people themselves and preserved in U.S. Government Bureau of American Ethnology reports. I have followed each legend with a short description of the homeland, culture, and beliefs of the tribe from which it came, so that a brief historical context is available to those who want it. These notes cannot do justice to the tribes in other than general ways, and do not attempt to characterize Native Americans of today.

Today, over 600 tribes and nations exist in the Americas, each with its own traditions, myths, and legends. This book purports to be only a taste of what these societies have to offer the children of the twenty-first century.

Toward the coming of the sun
There the people gathered,
And the great animals of every kind.

—Omaha

INTRODUCTION

Many thousands of years ago, tribes of nomadic peoples crossed a frozen corridor between polar ice caps called the Bering land bridge. This ancient bridge stretched from Siberia in Russia to what is now our northernmost state of Alaska, a distance of less than 60 miles. These nomads were the first immigrants to the New World. They were also the first Americans and the oldest race on earth.

Because there were no trees in this ice-filled world, nor bushes nor even plants for these early people to eat, they turned to the wild animals to feed their hunger. Over the frozen world they wandered, year after year, following the herds: woolly mammoths, bison, musk ox, and big horn elk. For weapons they fashioned knives, arrowheads, and spearheads out of stone and animal bones. These they shaped by skillful chipping, flake by flake, to create sharp-edged implements and practical tools. On and on the people wandered, generation after generation, following the animals, moving ever eastward toward the rising sun, carrying their worldly goods on their backs.

After many thousands of years, the ice that formed the gigantic glaciers began to melt. The frozen land bridge that once stretched from Siberia to Alaska flooded with water, isolating the people in this strange new world. Today we call this body of water the Bering Strait.

Descendants of these early nomads continued their migration. Some remained in the frozen northlands to become the present-day Eskimos, others wandered south, eventually spreading out into the four corners of what is now the United States. Here they divided into many tribes, some settling in the barren deserts of the Southwest. Some of these tribes became the Navajo, the Hopi, and the Pueblo nations. Others drifted eastward into the northern woodlands to become the Mohawk, the Seneca, and the Oneida. All these nomads were the great-great grandfathers of our American Indians.

Still others continued to wander, ever southward, into the continent of South America. As they roamed, some of these nomadic people settled down to become the highly advanced nations known as the Maya, the Toltec, the Aztec, and the Inca.

These early Americans could not have survived without the herds of wild animals. They needed their fur to keep warm. They needed their hides to protect their feet and build their shelters. They needed their meat to feed their children.

As they wandered southward and the climate became milder and the days warmer, the people began to supplement their food supply by collecting seeds, nuts, and berries. Later, when they learned to grow plants such as corn and squash, some of them settled down in permanent villages.

These Native Americans were dependent upon wild animals and plants, and they believed all things in nature were alive with a living, breathing, spirit. An animal was not just an animal, but an animal with a spirit. Water was not just water, but water with life. Even the mountains and trees and rocks were alive with a living spirit.

These early Americans had no written records, no books, and no schools. Knowledge of how to act and how to live was passed from generation to generation through the telling of ancient stories and legends. In the dark of long winter nights as the wind howled across the land, the people gathered together to hear their elders tell stories of how their world came to be.

These are the tales they told.

I make the world, and lo!

The world is finished.

Thus I make the world, and lo!

The world is finished.

Let it go,

Start it forth!

—Pima*

IN THE BEGINNING

ESKIMO

Before the dawn of time there were no people on earth. There were no animals, no birds, and no fish. There was nothing but ice and snow and the Great Western Sea.

One day Old-Man-Father-of-Fish looked about the empty land. All he saw was snow, miles and miles of ice and snow. He sat by the water and looked at the gray rocks along the shore. Then he looked out at the Great Western Sea, sparkling under the morning sun.

◆ ◆ ◆

* The Pima poem, originally sung and told orally by Chief Hovering Hawk, was recorded by Natalie Curtis Burlin in the early 1900s. The Father-of-Fish legend is common to native peoples of the far north from Alaska to Greenland.

"There should be creatures to fill this sea," he said. "Creatures that swim and jump and dive about in the waves. Creatures that will feed the people-yet-to-be."

He sat on a rock and he thought and he thought.

Then Old-Man-Father-of-Fish took out his knife and he began to whittle on a piece of driftwood. All day long he carved and he whittled, sending chip after chip flying into the sea.

"On-ja-ja-ja," he sang.

The chips began to squirm.

"Ja-ja-ja-ja," he chanted.

The chips began to twist.

"On-ja-ja-ja," he cried.

The chips turned into wiggling, squirming, fish.

"From henceforth you shall be Salmon," said Old-Man-Father-of-Fish.

Away swam Salmon far out into the waters of the Great Western Sea and disappeared under the rolling waves.

All night long Old-Man-Father-of-Fish carved and he whittled, sending chip after chip into the sea.

"On-ja-ja-ja," he sang.

The chips began to wiggle.

"Ja-ja-ja-ja," he chanted.

The chips began to squirm.

"On-ja-ja-ja," he cried.

The chips turned into more fish.

"Henceforth you shall be Char, and you," he said, "shall be Cod."

Char dived deep beneath the great blue waters and hid among the rocks.

Cod swam far out to sea.

All summer long Old-Man-Father-of-Fish sat on his rock and he carved.

All winter long Old-Man-Father-of-Fish sat on his rock and he whittled.

As he sat and as he whittled, chip after chip went flying into the sea. There they turned into fish.

"You shall be Halibut. You shall be Lumpsucker. And you," he said, "shall be Capelin."

On and on he went, carving and whittling and naming fish after fish.

When all the fish were created and all the fish were named, Old-Man-Father-of-Fish stood up and threw the last piece of driftwood out to sea, far out beyond the rolling waves.

"On-ja-ja-ja," he sang. "Ja-ja-ja-ja," he chanted. "You shall be the largest of all the creatures.

"I name you Whale."

And that is how Old-Man-Father-of-Fish filled the ocean with food for the people-yet-to-be.

❖❖❖❖❖❖❖❖❖❖❖❖❖❖❖❖❖❖❖❖❖❖❖❖❖

ABOUT THE ESKIMO

The Eskimo, or *Inuit* as they call themselves, are by necessity a hardy people. They live in a world of ice and snow, the coldest regions of North America. Their homelands, which extended across the Arctic Circle from Alaska to Greenland, were vaster than those of any other peoples in the world. To this day descendants of the early Eskimo still occupy these ancestral lands.

Neighboring Natives called these people "The Eskimo," a term meaning "those who eat their meat raw."

Historically, the Eskimo lived in small family groups, or bands. The availability of food determined the size of these bands. The Eskimo were skilled hunters and fishermen, constantly on the move in search of food. They used dogsleds for traveling and hauling heavy loads. On the land, they hunted birds, rabbits, wolves, foxes, and caribou. From the sea they gathered seals, walruses, whales, and fish. Their diet, which consisted almost entirely of fish and red meat with about 40 percent fat, was surprisingly healthy.

The Eskimo fashioned tools and weapons from animal bones, and used their sinew and hide for clothing, ropes, and for sewing. Children learned by working alongside adults.

Their summer shelters, made of animal hides stretched over driftwood or animal bones, were temporary and quickly built. In the winter they built snow houses called *igloos,* or oblong houses of wood or bone with snow or sod coverings.

The traditional religion of the Eskimo centered around their food supply. Among their many beliefs, they believed in *inuas,* or spirits, who determined the availability of fish and animals and where to hunt. They also believed that all things, living and nonliving, had souls, and the souls of game animals lived in their bladders. After a seal kill, the Eskimo inflated its bladder and threw it back into the sea. This, they believed, ensured the future supply of seals. They also returned whale and walrus skulls to the sea. During the dark winter months the elders held dances and told the ancient stories, such as this popular legend of how the fish came to be.

Earth Magician shapes this world.
Behold what he can do!
Round and smooth he molds it.
Behold what he can do.

—Pima

THE-TWO-MEN-WHO-CHANGED-THINGS

MAKAH

Before the beginning of time there was only Mother Earth and the Great Western Sea. There were no animals to wander about the land. There were no birds to fill the air with song.

There was only darkness and the fish that swam in the Great Western Sea.

The two brothers of Father Sun and Sister Moon came down to earth to prepare the world for the people-yet-to-be. Their names were *Ho-ho-e-ap-bess,* which means The-Two-Men-Who-Changed-Things.

They looked at the sea filled with fish.

They looked at the land filled with sand, miles and miles of sand. There were no trees, no green grass, no flowers, and no bushes.

They looked at the creatures that crawled the land, strange dark wiggly creatures that were neither animals nor birds.

"We need something to cover this land," said The-Two-Men-Who-Changed-Things.

They called all the wiggly creatures together.

They pointed at some of the creatures.

"Yo-oh-he-ya-yah," they chanted.

The creatures turned into green plants.

They pointed at other creatures.

"He-ya-yah," they sang.

The creatures turned into bushes.

One wiggly creature was especially nasty. "He steals our food," cried the other creatures.

The-Two-Men-Who-Changed-Things tied the creature's legs together. They tied his arms to his body. Then they threw him far out into the Great Western Sea.

"Yo-oh-he-yah," they chanted.

The creature turned into a seal.

"From this day forward," said The-Two-Men-Who-Changed-Things, "if you want to eat you must catch your own fish."

One of the creatures was a great fisherman. Around his shoulders he wore a little cape. Day after day he waded about the shallow waters spearing fish with a pointed stick.

"Yo-oh-he-ya-yah," chanted The-Two-Men-Who-Changed-Things. "You shall be Great Blue Heron."

They turned his cape into a mantle of beautiful feathers. They turned the stick into a sharp-pointed bill. Today you will find the great bird still wading about the shallow waters, hunting for fish.

Two of the wiggly creatures had huge appetites. They argued. They stole food. And they squawked. Day after day they argued and squawked.

The-Two-Men-Who-Changed-Things turned one of the creatures into Raven. They turned the other into Crow. To this day when you hear a "cr-r-r-r-e-uck," answered by a "ca-a-a-a-a-ash," you know Raven is squawking at Crow.

One water creature pointed to another and cried, "He took my necklace of shells."

"Then he shall be Kingfisher. Henceforth he shall search for food along the shore."

The-Two-Men-Who-Changed-Things asked another creature if he wanted to be a fish or a bird.

"Neither," answered the creature.

"Yo-oh-ha-ya-yah," they chanted. "You shall be Mink. You will live on land and eat fish that swim along the shore."

Then The-Two-Men-Who-Changed-Things looked at the land.

"The people-yet-to-be will need tough wood to make bows." They pointed to another creature. "You are tough and strong, you shall be Yew tree."

To another creature they said, "The people-yet-to-be will need slender shoots for arrows. You shall be Arrowwood. In the early summer you will be covered with beautiful white blossoms."

"Yo-oh-ha-ya-yah," they called to a huge fat creature.

"You shall be Cedar tree. The people-yet-to-be will need your wood to make canoes."

"You," they pointed to another creature, "shall be Spruce tree. When the north wind blows you will feed the fires that warm the houses of the people-yet-to-be."

They changed one creature with a cross temper into Crab Apple tree saying, "You shall always bear sour fruit."

They created Hemlock tree and Cherry tree. They turned one tough creature into Alder tree so the people-yet-to-be could make strong paddles for their canoes.

One after the other The-Two-Men-Who-Changed-Things changed each creature, some into birds, some into plants and trees, and others into animals.

All that was living grew and prospered.

And that is how our world was created for the people-yet-to-be.

❧ ● ❧ ● ❧ ● ❧ ● ❧ ● ❧ ● ❧ ● ❧ ● ❧ ● ❧ ● ❧ ● ❧ ● ❧ ● ❧ ● ❧ ●

ABOUT THE MAKAH

The Makah made their home in Cape Flattery, on the Olympic Peninsula in the present state of Washington. Living between the mountains and the sea, they called themselves "The People Who Lived on the Cape by the Rocks and the Sea Gulls."

Life for the Makah was abundantly rich and the climate was mild, warmed by moist Pacific currents. With the bounty provided by their homeland, the Makah were able to settle permanently in one place. From the sea they caught a variety of fish, especially salmon, as well as sea birds, seals, sea otters, and whales. They fashioned fishhooks and knives of stone and animal bones. The forests of cedar trees that surrounded them were filled with mountain goat, bear, deer, elk, and small animals, and there were roots and berries. Ducks, gulls, and geese swam in ponds filled with trout. From the cedar trees the Makah built houses large enough for twenty to forty people, or clans, and fashioned sea-going canoes, some as long as thirty-five feet.

They decorated their houses and canoes with realistic designs of animals and mythical characters. Traditional motifs such as Killer Whale, Raven, and Eagle were popular. Carved totem poles stood by the houses of important families. Women wove fabric on looms using wool and fur from mountain goats and hair from dogs, fluff from fireweed, and cattails mixed with wool, as well as the bark from the cedar tree. They also made combs and necklaces from shells. Both men and women wore clothing made from animal hides and cedar. When the rains came they wore beautifully decorated capes and conical-shaped hats.

The Makah believed their world was made up of three parts: the beach, the forest, and their homeland in between. To them, all existence was a cycle of birth, death, and rebirth. A whale might be a spirit in disguise, or an ancestor that had lived long ago. When a hunter killed an animal, he returned the bones to the sea or to the forest to ensure its rebirth.

Children learned how their world came to be through legends told by the elders.

Pleasant it looked,

This newly created world.

Along the length and breadth

Of the earth, the Earthmaker

Extended the green reflection.

It was pleasant to see.

—Winnebago*

THE EARTH DIVER

CREE

efore the dawn of time there were no people on the earth. All the animals and birds lived together in peace. They talked with one another like people.

One day as they sat talking and laughing, it began to rain.

Day after day it rained.

Night after night it rained.

Soon the lakes overflowed and the animals fled to the safety of the mountains.

◆ ◆ ◆

* Variations of this story are common to many Algonquin tribes and are often called by the name Earth Bearer.

On and on it rained until there was no land, no trees, and no mountains. Only water and water animals swimming around and around.

"I'm tired," complained Beaver.

"Keep swimming," cried Muskrat.

Around and around the animals swam, around and around and around.

"What are we going to do?" wailed Duck.

"Swim," said Beaver, "or you'll surely drown."

"There is earth beneath this water," said Turtle.

"Earth?" cried Beaver.

"Earth?" cried the animals.

"We must dive for some," said Muskrat.

"Who can dive that deep?" asked Loon.

"I will try," said Duck. He took a deep breath and down he went, down, down, down, pushing his paddle feet back and forth. Soon he was back. "It's too deep," he sputtered.

"Turtle," said Beaver, "You make your home beneath the water. You try."

Down went Turtle, moving his stubby legs up and down. He too came back. "It's so dark down there I lost my way."

"Loon, you're bigger. You try."

Down went Loon. He was gone so long the animals thought he had surely drowned. Then back up he came, gasping for air.

"Otter," they cried, "you are brave and strong. You try."

Down went Otter.

Back to the surface he floated, his feet all tangled up with seaweed.

"What's to become of us?" asked Muskrat.

"We'll all drown," cried the animals.

"I will try," said Beaver. Down he dove.

He too came back tired and out of breath. "There's nothing down there," he gasped, slapping the water with his flat tail.

"Try again," begged the animals.

Down, down, down, went Beaver. Soon he ran out of breath.

Back he came, shaking the water from his fur. "I reached the bottom and grabbed some dirt," he cried, "but I lost it coming up."

How the animals wept.

"Muskrat," they cried, "you are our last hope."

Down went Muskrat, but he didn't go deep enough.

Again he dove, deeper and deeper. Soon he was back, struggling for air.

"Try again," begged the animals.

Down went Muskrat a third time.

The animals waited and waited. "Surely he has drowned," they cried, as bubble after bubble floated back to the surface.

Then up came Muskrat.

In his paws was a tiny piece of dirt.

All the animals rejoiced.

They each took a speck of dirt from Muskrat's paw and placed it on top of Turtle's shell. There the dirt began to grow, piece by piece.

Day by day it grew.

Night by night it grew.

After many suns and many moons it grew and grew until it became the earth.

Then all the animals climbed up on the land and they rested.

And that is how Turtle became Earth Bearer, carrying the world around on his back. Down through time he walks about. Whenever he moves, huge waves form upon the seas. Whenever he is angry, great earthquakes spread across the land.

✦•

ABOUT THE CREE

The early Cree occupied a large part of Canada, from Saskatchewan to Quebec, and filtered down into the northern part of the United States. The western Cree were people of the Plains while the eastern Cree were woodland tribes. Small bands or clans lived and hunted together.

The Cree adapted to a wide variety of habitats. The western tribes depended on buffalo for food, and it is thought that they introduced the method of hunting by driving animals into enclosures. The eastern Cree depended on moose and elk, as well as on fish, ducks, geese, and other birds. They also hunted bear, rabbit, squirrel, wolf, lynx, muskrat, and gopher. Roots and berries were taken in season, as was syrup tapped from maple trees. The men hunted with bows and arrows and stone knives, and in battle they carried war clubs and hide-covered shields.

In summer, the eastern Cree traveled by birch bark canoe; in winter by sled. They also used snowshoes, which gave them a great advantage over their enemies. Dogs, and later horses, were used for hauling meat, firewood, and household equipment from one camp site to another.

The men wore leather breechcloths that hung down both front and back, decorated with beads and dyed quills. A buffalo robe covered them in cold weather. Women wore hide dresses that hung from the shoulders and were decorated sometimes with fringes. Both men and women wore leggings and moccasins made of leather. They also wore necklaces of animal teeth, bones, and claws.

Their houses were hide-covered tepees and their beds bundles of grass covered with buffalo robes. Household utensils were of bone, shell, and birch bark.

The Cree believed in the all-powerful god, *Kice Manito,* and in a variety of other supernatural spirits that manifested themselves as birds and animals. To appease these spirits they feasted and danced at ceremonies called *powwows.* They painted their faces and put on their finest clothing and ceremonial headdresses made of feathers and buffalo horns.

At age fifteen, the boys were sent into the forest alone for five days, without food or water, on a vision quest to find their own spirit helpers. They believed these spirits guarded and protected them through dreams and visions throughout their lives.

During the long, cold winter nights, children gathered around the elders to hear the tales of how their world came to be.

Behold; nearer comes
The ray of Father Sun.
It comes over all the land,
For us to touch,
And gives us strength.

—Pawnee

HOW RAVEN STOLE DAYLIGHT*

TLINGIT

In the beginning, a great cloud of darkness lay over Mother Earth. There was no sun, no moon, and no stars. The birds could not see to fly. The animals could not see to hunt.

Around and around the ground they stumbled, bumping into rocks and trees. They even bumped into each other.

"Watch where you're going," grumbled Fox as Coyote stepped on his tail.

◆ ◆ ◆

* This legend, with variations, is typical of the tales told by many Native peoples of the Northwest coast.

"How?" said Coyote, "I can't see."

"None of us can see," complained the animals. "We can't hunt for food and our children are hungry."

"I don't know if I'm eating grass or weeds," cried Deer.

"I can't find my way through the woods," grumbled Wolf.

"What can we do?" cried the animals.

"I have seen a light," said Owl.

"A light?" cried the birds.

"Where?" asked the animals.

"As I fly the night sky I have seen a light in the lodge of Daylight-Man."

"Where does Daylight-Man live?" asked Porcupine.

"In a lodge far beyond the mountains," said Owl. "There in a carved box he keeps a ball of light."

"Owl," said Porcupine, "your eyes see in the dark. You fly to the house of Daylight-Man and steal the ball of light."

"It's too far," complained Owl.

"Raven," cried the animals, "your wings are big and strong. You fly to the lodge of Daylight-Man."

Raven, with his snow-white feathers, was the most beautiful of all the birds. He looked at the animals. He looked at the birds. Then he looked at the animal children. He saw they were starving.

"I will try," said Raven.

He spread his beautiful white wings and off he flew into the black night. But it was so dark he soon lost his way. On he flew, following the sound of water from a river below.

"Ca-a-a-a-a," he cried, pushing his wings faster and faster.

"Ca-a-a-a-a," echoed the mountains and valleys.

Up over rocky cliffs flew Raven. There in the distance he saw a glimmer of light hidden among the dark clouds. On and on he flew, following the light, until he came to the lodge of Daylight-Man.

Beside the lodge, Daylight-Man's daughter knelt by a stream.

Raven changed himself into a tiny leaf of the cedar tree. Then out he floated on the water. Daylight-Man's daughter dipped a woven basket into the water and began to drink. As she drank, she swallowed the leaf.

After a while she gave birth to a child, who was really Raven.

Daylight-Man was delighted with the child and called the Boy-Who-Was-Raven, grandson. He laughed with the child and played with him as he crawled about the floor.

The Boy-Who-Was-Raven didn't want to crawl about or play games. He wanted the sacred box that held the ball of light. Around and around the lodge he crawled, searching for the box. He looked in all the corners. He looked under the windows. He looked inside wooden chests.

But he did not find the ball of light.

Then he looked up at the shelves.

There it was, a beautifully carved box sitting high on the shelf.

"Wa-a-a-a," wailed the Boy-Who-Was-Raven, pointing to the box.

"What does the boy want?" asked Daylight-Man.

"Wa-a-a-a-a-a," yelled the Boy-Who-Was-Raven, louder and louder.

"He wants the box of light," said Daylight-Man's daughter.

"Give it to him," said Daylight-Man.

Daylight-Man's daughter reached for the sacred box and opened it. She took out the ball of light and gave it to the Boy-Who-Was-Raven.

"He-e-e-e-e," laughed the Boy-Who-Was-Raven. Around and around the room he rolled the ball of light. "He-e-e-e-e," he giggled.

As he crawled about the floor he watched Daylight-Man. As he rolled the ball around he watched Daylight-Man's daughter.

As soon as Daylight-Man and Daylight-Man's daughter were asleep, he grabbed the ball of light, put it in the box, and slammed the lid shut. He changed himself back into Raven. Seizing the box in his powerful talons, he flew up through the smokehole of the lodge and back into the night sky.

Over trees and cliffs he went. Over fields and running waters. On and on he flew until he came to the top of the highest mountain. There he opened the box. As the ball of light escaped into the sky it become the sun, and its blinding flash burned Raven's feathers from head to tail.

And that is why ravens are black, even to this day.

ABOUT THE TLINGIT

The name Tlingit—pronounced "Klēn-kit" or "Tlēn-git"—means "The People." They lived along the Pacific Coast and nearby islands and estuaries in what is today southern Alaska and northern

British Columbia. Like their distant neighbors, the Makah, they believed the earth was made up of three parts: the beach, the forest, and the land in between, where they lived.

Life was good for the Tlingit. The ocean they fished held an abundance of fish as well as seals and whales. Warm ocean currents provided them with a mild climate. Mountain goats, bear, and deer roamed their forests, supplying them with food and clothing. The inner bark fiber from cedar, spruce, and cypress trees, which the women softened by pounding, was cut into strips and combined with mountain goat wool to produce yarn that was used for weaving. The trees that surrounded their villages also gave them fuel to burn and wood to build their houses and dugout canoes.

Several families, or clans, lived together in large cedar lodges which they painted with colorful pictures of animals and birds. They carved and decorated totem poles, and each clan placed a totem pole in front of its house. The animal and bird carvings on the pole told of that family's history. They also carved beautiful bowls, cooking utensils, and ceremonial masks to ward off evil spirits.

Like the Makah, the Tlingit believed in a supreme god that lived in the sky, and in spirit helpers who controlled such things as the weather, hunting, and even sickness. The shaman, or medicine man, held the power to contact these spirits.

During the long dark winter months, families gathered together for the telling of ancient stories and legends, and of how their world came to be. For these ceremonies they wore hand-carved masks and colorful robes. In this manner the elders passed down to the children the values of right and wrong and how to live.

Oh, youthful Dawn, we see you come!

Brighter shines your glowing light

As nearer you come,

To bring us life.

—Pawnee

WHY WE HAVE DAY AND NIGHT

MAIDU

As soon as Raven* threw the ball of light into the sky, night escaped over the mountains and disappeared into the Great Western Sea. There it stayed, hiding its face from the heat of the sun.

Day after day the great ball of light smiled upon the earth.

Or was it night after night?

The animals were confused. They didn't know when

◆ ◆ ◆

* Raven made his home throughout the land, and he appears in the myths and legends of many tribes, sometimes as the hero, other times as the trickster.

to hunt. They didn't know when to eat. They didn't know when to sleep.

"We need darkness to hunt," complained Bobcat.

"We need light to find our food," said Deer.

"Night is best for hunting," argued Bear.

"We need light to feed our children," sang the birds.

"Night! We must have night!" squeaked Bat.

Back and forth the animals argued.

Back and forth the birds chattered.

"Some of you want light," said Chipmunk, "others want darkness. Why not have both? Half the time daylight, the other half night. Then you will know when to hunt, when to eat, and when to sleep." He began to sing:

> *"Let darkness come,*
> *But we must have light."*

This made Bear angry. "No," he cried, and he began to shout:

> *"Darkness is best,*
> *We must have night."*

Then Bear turned and chased after Chipmunk. Around and around they ran up hills and over rocks. As Chipmunk scurried up a tree, Bear reached out and scratched his sharp claws down the little animal's back.

And that is why Chipmunk has black lines on his back, even to this day.

Louder and louder sang the birds.

Louder and louder shouted the animals.

As they argued and as they shouted, dark clouds billowed high in the eastern sky.

On and on the animals argued and on and on the birds squawked as the clouds grew bigger and bigger.

From the west, the sun sent its most powerful rays across the sky, but the oncoming clouds swallowed them up.

Darker and darker grew the sky.

Weaker and weaker grew the rays of the sun.

When the dark clouds reached the western rim of the sky, the sun dropped behind the mountains and night fell silently across the land.

And that is why we have both day and night.

✦•✦•✦•✦•✦•✦•✦•✦•✦•✦•✦•✦•✦•✦•✦•✦•✦•✦•✦•

ABOUT THE MAIDU

The Maidu Indians lived along the eastern tributaries of the Sacramento River, on the eastern slopes of the Sierra Nevada mountains in what is today northern California. The name Maidu means "person."

Life for the Maidu was relatively easy in the mild climate of California. Families, or clans, grouped together in small villages of about a hundred people. Their houses were either earth-covered, domed pit houses, sometimes as large as 40 feet in diameter or huts made of poles covered with tule mats and brush. Being a seed-gathering people, the Maidu were semi-nomadic, journeying from their homes in search of acorns and other nuts, seeds, wild plants, and a variety of grasses. They dug roots and bulbs from the ground, and harvested kelp and seaweed from the ocean, which they boiled for soup or dried and stored in beautifully coiled and twined baskets. The men hunted rabbits, quail, and gophers, and fished for salmon.

What clothing they wore, aprons or breechcloths, the women made from plant fiber and animal hides decorated with abalone shells and feathers. The Maidu engaged in little warfare with neighboring tribes as there was enough food for all.

The Maidu believed in a single deity, *Chareya,* or "Old Man," as creator of the land and all the plants and animals. The men gathered in sweat lodges for ceremonials that centered around the worship of ancestral ghosts. Boys and girls attended initiation ceremonials that included both religious and moral instruction as well as stories about how their world came to be.

I have made the stars!

I have made the stars!

Above the earth I threw them.

All things above I've made

And placed them for the people.

—Pima

THE STAR CHILDREN

NAVAJO

When the world was still new, Black-God, the Lord-of-the-Dark, crossed the night sky. When he reached the western rim of the world he entered the hogan of Earth and Sky. On the floor sat Brother Coyote, licking his paws.

"Why are you sitting here inside your hogan?" asked Black-God.

"It is so dark outside I get lost," said Sky.

"I can't see where I'm going," complained Earth.

"Come outside with me," said Black-God. "I will give you light."

Out into the dark went Sky and Earth, followed by Coyote.

"Watch," said Black-God and he held out his leg. Tied to one of his ankles was a small group of stars.

Black-God wiggled his leg. Up jumped the stars to his knee.

Again he bounced his leg. Up jumped the stars to his hip.

Earth and Sky laughed and clapped their hands.

Then the Lord-of-the-Dark took a deep breath and stomped both legs. Up jumped the stars to his shoulder.

Again he stomped. Up jumped the stars to his left temple.

"Stay," he commanded.

Today, if you look closely, you can still see the stars twinkling on Black-God's temple. The people call them the *Dilyehe* (the Pleiades).

"What have you there?" asked Brother Coyote pointing to Black-God's deerskin pouch.

Black-God opened the bag. He took out a handful of white crystals.

"Watch," he said.

He reached up and placed each crystal constellation across the night sky. There was Man-with-Feet-Ajar (Vorus). Then Horned-Rattler, Bear, and Thunder. In the south he placed First-Big-One (Scorpio). To the north he placed Polar-Star (North Star). Then he stretched his arm across the sky and placed Revolving-Male (Big Dipper) and Revolving-Female (Little Dipper).

As Brother Coyote watched, Black-God took out a big crystal and placed Slender-First-One (Orion) high above their heads.

"Now I can see where I'm going," laughed Sky.

"Now I can see through the night," smiled Earth.

Last of all, Black-God took out some crystal dust. He waved his hand across the sky and spread out the Milky Way.

When that was done, Black-God rested.

As soon as Black-God closed his eyes, Brother Coyote grabbed his pouch. He took a deep breath and blew the remaining crystal dust across the sky, filling the night with twinkling stars. Then he took out the brightest crystal of all and threw it into the southern sky.

To this day the people call this star the Coyote Star.

Every night before going to sleep they look toward the southern sky.

There they see Coyote, winking back at them.

◆•◆

ABOUT THE NAVAJO

The Navajos called themselves the *Din'é,* which means "The People." They lived in northern Arizona and New Mexico, as well as in southern Utah and Colorado, within what they called the four sacred mountains. They named their land *Dinetah.*

Today, the Navajo comprise the largest Indian tribe in North America. The Navajo traditionally did not live in villages, but in small scattered family groups on land sufficient for farming. Their homes, or hogans, were made of supporting poles or of logs chinked with mud and bark. Their doorways always faced east in order to greet the morning sun. The men hunted deer, mountain sheep, antelope, and rabbits for food and clothing. In addition they raised domesticated sheep and goats for meat, milk, and wool.

Navajo clothing changed over the centuries, but more recently, the men wore cotton shirts and pants and the women wore long colorful skirts and soft cotton blouses. In the last hundred years, the silver and turquoise jewelry of Navajo craftsmen has become popular. Rug and blanket weaving are also notable crafts.

A Navajo grandmother was the center of family life. All children belonged to her and to her clan. They were taught proper behavior through legends and by working alongside their elders.

The Navajo believed their early ancestors traveled upward through the earth, passing through different worlds with the help of mysterious spiritual beings. Upon arriving in this world, they knew that here they could live in harmony with the earth. They called this *hozho,* the Navajo Way, where everything was in balance and all things were interrelated. If this balance was disturbed, evil, sickness, and other dangers resulted. To restore order, "singers" conducted ceremonies called *chantways,* believing the *Yei,* or Holy Ones, were attracted by songs and prayers. If the *Yei* were pleased, balance was restored. Sand paintings and stories, as well as prayers and songs, were part of the *chantway.*

There hangs the moon
Eating her fruit
And throwing the peels
Into the lake.

—*Aztec**

PRINCESS
GOLDEN BELLS

n the beginning the Great Mother, Coatlique, stood at the entrance to her cave.

"My children," she called out to the twinkling stars. "I have made you each a god that you may shine for the glory of the earth children."

The stars looked down.

They listened to their mother.

❖ ❖ ❖

* The Aztec poem is a popular nursery rhyme in Mexico to this day. I heard it, and the legend of Princess Golden Bells, many times while living in Mexico.

"Soon I will bring forth another child," she said, " a man child. He will be the most powerful of all my children."

The star children were angry. A new brother with power greater than theirs?

"This must not happen," they cried.

"What can we do?" they asked one another.

"We must kill our mother," said the star brothers.

"No," cried golden-haired Coyolxauqui, or Princess Golden Bells as she was called. She was the most beautiful of all the star children.

Off she ran to warn her mother.

The star brothers ran after her.

As Princess Golden Bells approached the cave, the Great Mother gave birth to the new child. He was truly a god, for he sprang forth armed and fully grown. The Great Mother named him Maxilla, God of War, Lord of the Mighty Aztecs.

Hearing the footsteps of his brothers, Maxilla rushed out to protect his mother. At that instant Princess Golden Bells arrived at the opening to the cave.

"Mother, Mother," she cried out, "take cover. My brothers are. . ."

But Maxilla released his darts and Princess Golden Bells fell dead at his feet.

When the star brothers saw Princess Golden Bells fall, they feared this mighty brother. Back to the sky they fled never to return to earth again.

The Great Mother wept for her beautiful daughter. She told Maxilla of the goodness of his sister's heart. She told him of her love.

With a great roar the mighty god knelt beside his sister's body. With one blow of his ax he cut off her head. Seizing the long golden hair in his hands, he threw the head with all his might up, up, far up, into the highest heavens.

There it stayed, glowing with its special beauty.

Maxilla named it the moon.

To this day you can see the princess shining in the night sky. If you look closely you can see the golden bells glowing on her cheeks.

◆ ● ◆ ● ◆ ● ◆ ● ◆ ● ◆ ● ◆ ● ◆ ● ◆ ● ◆ ● ◆ ● ◆ ● ◆ ● ◆ ● ◆ ● ◆ ● ◆ ● ◆ ● ◆ ● ◆ ●

ABOUT THE AZTEC

The Aztec were one of the most powerful people of ancient America. The Valley of Mexico was their home, but their military power extended as far north as the southern United States, eastward from the Pacific to the Gulf of Mexico, and south into the Yucatan Peninsula and Guatemala. Their capital Tenochtitlan, present-day Mexico City, had a population of well over 100,000 inhabitants.

Ordinary families lived in simple adobe houses with thatched roofs. The more powerful and wealthy had palaces with many rooms. Men worked the fields of corn, a plant that originated in ancient Mexico, and raised beans, squash, chili, tomatoes, cocoa plants for chocolate, peppers, avocadoes, potatoes, tobacco, hemp. They also domesticated small dogs and turkeys. Women managed the household, spending much of their time grinding corn on concave stones called *metates* to make meal for tortillas. They made clothing from cotton and the fiber of the century plant. Powerful chiefs wore tunics of coyote fur, feathers, and dyed cotton. Men of lesser social rank wore breechcloths, capes, and sandals while the women dressed in ankle-length skirts and sleeveless, plain white blouses. They crafted beautiful pottery and ornaments made of gold, silver, and jade.

The Aztec had a system of writing called hieroglyphics and they recorded history, geography, religion, poetry, public events, and calendars. Children attended schools conducted by *sacerdotes,* or religious leaders.

The men were fearless warriors under a strong military government. They fought with bows and arrows and obsidian-tipped swords and clubs. They wore helmets and armor of thick quilted cotton and carried shields.

The Aztec worshiped many gods, gods who controlled every aspect of their lives from birth to death. Each god required his or her own special ceremony, with its prayers and sacrifices. The Aztec built huge, flat-topped pyramids of stone, which may still be seen in the central plaza in Mexico City, to honor these gods.

That wind, that wind

Shakes my tipi, shakes my tipi,

And sings songs for me,

And sings songs for me.

—Kiowa

ORIGIN OF THE WIND

HOPI

During the time of our great-grandfathers, Wind-God blew his mighty breath over Mother Earth. Trees bent before his great power and the world trembled. Animals hid in their dens. Birds stayed in their nests.

"W-h-o-o-o-o," howled Wind-God, day after day.

"W-h-o-o-o-o," wailed Wind-God, night after night.

One day the two war gods, both named Little Fellow, walked up a hillside to visit old Grandmother Spider.

"W-h-o-o-o-o," cried Wind-God.

He tugged at their hair. He tugged at their clothes. He tugged at their feet. Then he took a deep breath and blew them back down the hill.

"Ow-w-w-w-w-w," howled Little Fellow.

"Ow-w-w-w-w-w," howled Little Fellow.

"W-h-o-o-o-o," laughed Wind-God.

"We must stop Wind-God," cried Little Fellow.

"How?" asked Little Fellow. "We can't see him. We can't touch him. How can we stop him?"

"We will ask Grandmother Spider."

Back up the hill crawled the two Little Fellows and into Grandmother Spider's house. Grandmother Spider was busy cooking cornmeal mush.

"Grandmother," cried Little Fellow, rubbing the bumps on his sore arms. "Wind-God is after us."

"Grandmother," cried Little Fellow, rubbing the bruises on his sore legs. "How can we stop Wind-God from hurting us?"

"You must do as I say," said Grandmother Spider.

She scooped up some of the cornmeal, wrapped it in a pouch, and gave it to the Little Fellows. She pointed to a distant mountain far off in the land of the setting sun.

"Take this pouch of cornmeal to the big crack in black rock, deep inside Sunset Mountain. There you'll find the home of Wind-God."

Off went the Little Fellows toward Sunset Mountain carrying the pouch of cornmeal mush. Day after day they walked, pushing against Wind-God's breath. Night after night they walked, pushing against Wind-God's power.

On the fourth day they came to the foot of Sunset Mountain.

"W-h-o-o-o-o," howled Wind-God through the crack in black rock, "g-o-o-a-w-a-a-a-y-y." He took a deep breath and blew, sending the Little Fellows tumbling across the land.

Back crawled the Little Fellows on their hands and knees, back to the foot of Sunset Mountain.

"W-h-o-o-o-o-o," laughed Wind-God, blowing harder and harder.

The Little Fellows got down on their stomachs. They wiggled up to the crack in black rock. There they took out Grandmother Spider's sticky cornmeal mush and stuffed it into the crack.

And the wind stopped.

"W-h-o-o-o-o-o," blew Wind-God against the rock.

But the cornmeal mush had sealed Wind-God's door shut.

"W-h-o-o-o-o-o-o," he blew, harder and harder.

The door held fast.

A quiet peace spread over Mother Earth. Nothing stirred, not a blade of grass, not a leaf, not even a grain of sand. Out came the animals from their dens. Overhead birds filled the air with song.

Back from Sunset Mountain came the Little Fellows laughing and dancing.

Father Sun smiled down upon Mother Earth.

Day after day he smiled.

The land turned hotter and hotter.

There was no wind to cool the air.

There were no clouds to hide the sun.

There were only waves and waves of shimmering heat dancing across the land. The corn in the fields turned brown and the rivers dried up.

The animals complained of the heat and returned to their dens.

The birds complained of the heat and flew back to their nests.

The Little Fellows complained of the heat and hid behind black rock. "The hot sand burns my feet," they cried.

"This heat is worse than the wind," said Little Fellow.

"We must make peace with Wind-God," said Little Fellow.

Back to Sunset Mountain went the Little Fellows. There they removed a tiny speck of cornmeal mush from the crack in black rock. They left a hole just big enough for Wind-God to breathe through, but not big enough for his cruel breath to escape.

Out through the hole came a cool breeze.

Clouds appeared in the western sky. Over the land they floated, over the nests of the birds, and over the dens of the animals. The corn in the fields stood tall. The rivers danced along the rocks.

And that is why today only gentle breezes cross the land of the Hopi.

ABOUT THE HOPI

The name Hopi is a shortening of their word *Hopituh* meaning "Peaceful Ones." Like the present-day Hopi, these forebears made their home in the dry, desert areas of northeastern Arizona. In spite of the heat and lack of rain, they survived comfortably on high barren mesas, or tablelands.

A Hopi community lived in stone or adobe cliff-like pueblos, or villages, unique to this country. These pueblos were complex structures attached wall-to-wall with one another, with additional buildings on top. They did not have doors and people entered through an opening in the roof and climbed down notched logs. A series of ladders provided access to the upper houses. Men provided the building materials, but the women shaped them into houses. One of these pueblos, Oraibi, is the oldest continuously inhabited village in the United States.

In spite of the dry desert climate, the Hopi were excellent farmers. Women owned the houses and crops, and their most important crop was corn. They also raised squash, pumpkins, gourds, several kinds of beans, cotton, and tobacco, and gathered roots, leaves, berries, nuts, seeds, and wild onion. They domesticated turkeys, and the men were skilled hunters of deer, antelope, squirrels, rabbits, and other small game. They used the bones for tools and the sinew for bowstrings.

The Hopi made clothing and moccasins from cotton and animal hides. The men wore short tunics, moccasins, and leggings of cotton or hide. Women wore knee-length dresses that hung from their shoulders. Both men and women wore their hair fringed at the sides, and unmarried girls wore their hair in elaborate twists called "squash blossoms" over either ear. They also wore ornaments of shell, beads, and turquoise. The Hopi have been expert silversmiths, weavers, potters, and basketmakers for a long time.

Their religion, often referred to as "the Hopi Way," viewed everything in relationship to everything else. Birds and animals, as well as people, were all connected. They believed that Grandmother Spider and *Tawa,* the Sky God, created the earth. Grandmother Spider then divided the people into clans and sent them to live in different places. Guardian spirits, called *kachinas,* came to help the Hopi clans. They taught the people how to hunt and plant crops, how to gather firewood, and how to perform the ceremonies that would keep them in harmony with these spirits. Hopi children learn the traditions of their people through *kachinas.*

Where the wind is blowing,
The wind is roaring
I stand.
Westward the wind is blowing
The wind is roaring
I stand.

—*Teton Sioux*

SPRING DEFEATS WINTER*

SENECA

During the Big Sleep in the cold north country, there once lived an old giant. He was a very big giant with long white hair. His beard was covered with frost and icicles hung from his clothing.

◆ ◆ ◆

* The legend of Old Man Winter is common to the mythology of all the Eastern Woodland tribes, including the Iroquois, Seneca, Oneida, and others.

His name was Old-Man-Winter the Cold-Maker.

He ruled over a world without flowers, or grass, or running water. Only ice and snow and howling blizzards. Even his lodge was built of ice and snow.

Whenever he walked about, ice groaned and snow began to fall. Animals hid in their burrows and the land slept.

Old-Man-Winter's only friend was North Wind. Together they sat through the long dark days and freezing nights in Old-Man-Winter's lodge. They talked and laughed and smoked their pipes.

They listened to the driving snowflakes beating against the walls of the lodge. They heard the cry of the wind howling across the frozen land.

"He-e-e-e-e," laughed Old-Man-Winter. "I have brought so much snow the animals cannot feed their young."

"W-h-o-o-o-o-o," laughed North Wind. "I have sent so many winds whirling across the land that great trees bend before my power."

One morning as Old-Man-Winter and North Wind were sitting and smoking and talking and laughing, the wind stopped blowing.

The land was quiet.

Too quiet.

No whisper of falling snow touched the ground. No racket of howling wind shook the lodge. No sound of sleet or hail filled the air.

Old-Man-Winter peeked outside.

The snowdrifts were melting.

The ice on the rivers was melting.

Beside his door stood a young man with red cheeks and a smile on his face. Around his forehead was a wreath of sweet grass. In his hand he carried flowers.

"Go away," howled North Wind.

Old-Man-Winter was not afraid of the stranger. His magic was too strong. He invited the young man into the lodge. He gave him a pipe to smoke.

"Who are you?" demanded Old-Man-Winter.

"Why have you come?" demanded North Wind.

"My name is Spring," said the young man. As he spoke a gentle breeze filled the lodge.

This made Old-Man-Winter angry. "I am mightier than you," he cried. "When I blow my breath, waters freeze and snows fall. Even animals hide from my power."

North Wind blew his breath at the young stranger.

Old-Man-Winter blew his breath at the young stranger. But the harder he blew the warmer he became. Soon great tears poured from his eyes. Sweat rolled down his brow. The icicles on his clothing melted.

"Do you not know me, old man?" smiled the young stranger. "I bring warmth and sunshine to the land. Listen," he said, "listen to the song of South Wind pushing against your lodge."

"W-h-o-o-o-o-o-o," shrieked North Wind, and out the door he blew, back to the land of ice and snow.

Again and again Old-Man-Winter blew his breath at the young stranger, but nothing came from his mouth, not even a whisper.

Old-Man-Winter's long beard began to melt.

Harder and harder he blew.

Faster and faster his clothing melted.

Soon there was nothing left of Old-Man-Winter but a huge puddle of water on the floor of the lodge.

Once again Spring had defeated Old-Man-Winter.

ABOUT THE SENECA

The Seneca of old occupied the inland forests of the Allegheny River basin, in what is today upstate New York. They called themselves the "Great Hill People." They lived in close proximity to other tribes, and were constantly on the warpath with them. It was the Mohawk peacemaker of legend, Hiawatha,* who helped them form the federation known as the League of the Iroquois. This league originally consisted of five tribes: the Seneca, the Onondaga, the Cayuga, the Oneida, and the Mohawk. The Tuscarora later joined as the sixth tribe.

Instead of going to war with one another, tribal leaders gathered together in ceremonial longhouses. There, delegates from each tribe sat down to negotiate their differences. This league so impressed Benjamin Franklin that due to his admiration parts of the Constitution of the United States reflect its ideals.

The Seneca lived in large fortified villages. Several families, headed by a clan mother, lived in longhouses made of elm bark. The women raised corn, potatoes, beans, and squash, and gathered berries. The men were fierce warriors who fit their bowstrings with

✦ ✦ ✦

* Not to be confused with Henry Wadsworth Longfellow's romantic Ojibway hero.

poisoned arrows. They were also skilled hunters of deer, moose, fox, and mink, as well as ducks, geese, eagles, and hawks. They wore breechcloths and moccasins made of leather. The women wore ornaments of beads, shells, and bones over skirts that wrapped around their waists. They carried their infants on their backs wrapped in cradleboards.

The Seneca held great reverence for the three cosmic zones: the Upper World (sky and sun), the Earth, and the Under World (water, or beneath the earth). They believed in a creator, *Gitche Manito,* and in the natural power of creativity, or spirits, for all things. They devoted their energies to pleasing these spirits, both friendly and unfriendly.

There is a voice above,
The voice of Thunder.
Again and again it sounds,
Thonah! Thonah!
—Navajo

THE THEFT OF FIRE

uring the Moon When Wild Geese Fly, Old-Man-Winter the Cold-Maker blew his icy breath across the Mother Earth.

"W-h-o-o-o-o-o-o," he howled.

"W-h-o-o-o-o-o-o," answered North Wind.

The trees shed their leaves and the land turned brown. Soon deep snows covered the land. The animals shivered in their burrows and birds trembled in their nests.

There was no fire to keep them warm.

Only Thunder had fire. But he lived far away, high above the highest clouds.

On dark nights when Thunder threw his lightning bolts of fire across the sky the animals watched and shivered.

43

"We must steal that fire," cried Opossum.

"How?" asked the animals.

Back and forth the birds talked.

Back and forth the animals argued.

"Raven," said Eagle, "you're strong. You fly to Thunder's house and steal the fire."

"You're bigger," said Raven, "you try."

"No bird can fly beyond the sky," said Wise Old Owl.

As they talked and as they argued, a bolt of lightning flashed across the sky. Down it came, zigzagging toward Mother Earth. There it burned a hollow in a sycamore tree growing on an island in Great Water. It set the tree on fire.

"Fire!" cried the birds.

"Fire!" cried the animals.

"How can we get some?" asked Fox.

"Beaver, you live in the water, you try."

"The fire will burn my mouth," cried Beaver. "It will burn my fur."

"I will try," said Raven, "I am large and strong."

Raven spread his golden wings and away he flew, across the water to the sycamore tree. The fire was so hot it scorched his body from head to tail, turning his feathers black. Back he came without the fire. To this day Raven is black.

"Screech Owl, you are wise. You try," begged the council.

Away flew Screech Owl. As he peeked down into the hollow tree, a blast of fire scorched his eyes. Back he came without the fire. To this day Screech Owl's eyes are red. That is why he sees only in the dark.

Then Hoot Owl and Horned Owl flew off to the sycamore tree. Up burst a cloud of ashes leaving white rings round their eyes. They too came back without the fire. To this day they have white feathers around their eyes.

"I will try," said Little Racer, the snake.

"You?" laughed the animals.

"How?" tittered the birds.

Off went Little Racer swishing through the water. Up through the grass he wiggled and into a hole at the bottom of the sycamore tree. But the fire was so hot it burned his body black. Back he squirmed out through the hole and into the water. To this day that is why he wiggles back and forth as if trying to escape from fire.

"Watch me," said a large snake. His name was Climber because he always climbed up trunks of trees.

Up the burning tree he climbed. He poked his head down the hollow. The smoke was so strong it choked him. Into the fire he tumbled and was scorched. To this day he is called Great Black Snake.

"What are we to do?" cried the birds.

"What will become of us?" wailed the animals.

Back and forth the birds chattered.

Back and forth the animals argued.

"Bear, you go."

"I can't swim," said Bear. "You go."

"You go," cried the animals, pointing at the birds.

"No," shouted the birds. "You're bigger, you go."

Little Water Spider listened to the animals. She heard the cry of the birds. "I will go," she said.

"You?" laughed Bear. "How?"

"I can run on top of the water," said Water Spider.

"How will you carry the fire?" asked the animals.

"Watch," said Water Spider.

From her body she spun a long silken thread. Then she took the thread and wove it into a tiny, round *tusti* bowl. She fastened the bowl to her back.

Off she scurried across the water. Through the grass she climbed until she came to the sycamore tree.

The animals watched as Water Spider put a piece of coal into her *tusti* bowl. Then back across the water she scampered carrying the lump of burning coal.

How the animals cheered!

How the birds chattered!

And that is how the world got fire.

And that is why Water Spider still carries a little *tusti* bowl on her back, even to this day.

◆•◆

ABOUT THE CHEROKEE

The Cherokee lived in the Southern Appalachians in what is today North and South Carolina, Kentucky, Tennessee, northwest Georgia, and northern Alabama. They called themselves the *Ani-yun-wiya*, meaning "Real People." When Europeans came to the land, they were the largest tribe in this region.

The Cherokee lived in large villages and farmed along waterways. They built houses of poles covered with twigs and clay. The women grew corn, squash, pumpkins, beans, melons, sunflowers, and tobacco. The men fished and hunted turkey, bear, deer, and opossum with bows and arrows, and smaller game with blow guns.

A boy became a man only upon proving his courage as a hunter and a warrior.

Two chiefs governed each village: a war chief and one whose functions were peaceful. These could be either men or women. The war chief (red chief) was in charge of the lacrosse games that played an important role in the ceremonial life of the clans. For dress, both men and women wore buckskin and fiber clothing, moccasins, body paint, and ornaments.

In 1838-1839, the tribe was forced from their homelands by the United States Army and herded to the sparsely populated area of what is today Oklahoma. Thus began the tragic migration which the Cherokee called "The Trail Where We Cried," and known today as "The Trail of Tears." It is estimated that as many as a quarter of these Indians died of disease, starvation, exposure, and hardship while on the march, and more afterwards. Some Cherokee hid in the mountains and became the eastern band that now lives in North Carolina.

The Cherokee believed in an all-powerful spirit they called Master of Breath, who created man from the clay. They also believed in the spirits of air and earth, plants and animals.

At the center of each village was a circular council house where the men held religious rituals that had to do with the planting and gathering of crops, hunting, and warfare. During the ceremonies they smoked tobacco, believing the smoke carried their prayers skyward, up to Master of Breath. Their most important deity was the sun.

You are a spirit,

I am making you a spirit,

In the place where I sit,

I am making you a spirit.

—Chippewa

THE FIRST MAN

OSAGE

In the beginning of time there were no people on earth. No laughter filled the air. No sound of talking drums. No rhythm of dancing feet. And no games to please the gods. There were only birds and animals and fish that swam in the waters of the Great Western Sea.

Day after day Father Sun walked the bright sky. Night after night Sister Moon spread out her veil of stars.

But the days were empty.

The nights were quiet.

One day as Father Sun walked the sky, a small snail climbed out of the water and up the bank of a muddy stream. He sat in the sun and rested. As he sat and as he rested the stream began to rise. Higher and higher came the waters until they touched the bottom of Snail's shell.

Snail crept up onto a log.

Still higher came the waters, pulling the log out into the swirling stream. Around and around went Snail. Up and down bounced the log. Soon it came to Old Muddy Water, the river we now call the Missouri, a word that means "People Who Have Dugout Canoes."

There, the waters began to fall. Snail wiggled up onto the muddy riverbank and rested.

Day after day Father Sun smiled upon the land.

The air turned hotter and hotter.

The water turned hotter and hotter.

Snail turned hotter and hotter.

Suddenly his shell cracked wide open.

Out poked his head and two eyes.

Arms grew out of his body.

Hands grew out of his arms.

Legs grew out of his body.

Feet grew out of his legs.

He was no longer Snail.

He was Man and he was hungry.

Then the Great Spirit came to him.

He took Man into the forest and taught him how to make bows and arrows. He showed Man how to catch fish and clams along the riverbank. And he taught Man how to build a fire and roast meat.

Man sat down beside the fire and ate and ate until his hunger was satisfied.

"Go away, Man," called out Beaver, slapping the water with his tail. "This river belongs to me."

"No," said Man, "this river belongs to me."

And so they quarreled, each telling the other to go away.

As they quarreled Beaver's daughter came out of Beaver's house. How beautiful she looked with her dark hair and white teeth.

Man looked at her. He looked at her beautiful hair. He looked at her beautiful teeth. He liked her.

"This river is big enough for both of us," Man said to Beaver. "If you give me your daughter you may keep half of it."

So Man married Beaver's daughter and they became the parents of the Osage tribe.

To this day, no Osage will hurt a beaver, for they are brothers.

* *

ABOUT THE OSAGE

The Osage were a powerful, well-organized people of the Plains. They lived in the present states of Kansas, Missouri, and Illinois, along the Osage River, a tributary of the Missouri River. They called themselves *Ni-u-ko'n-ska,* "Children of the Middle Waters."

In the middle 1800s the U.S. government forced the tribe onto a small reservation in Oklahoma where the Osage now live. The later discovery of oil on these lands has made them the richest tribe in the United States.

Most of the year the Osage lived in small villages along the river where the women raised corn, beans, and squash in its rich top soil. They also made tools and household utensils, and sewed their clothing. Families lived in oval or rectangular lodges made of woven mats or skins and covered with earth, supported by a wooden framework. A short time each year, when following the migrating herds of buffalo, they lived in tepees.

Men were the hunters and warriors. They used bows and arrows and stone-tipped lances for hunting deer, buffalo, elk, and small game. They wore deerskin breechcloths or aprons and leggings while the women wore a cape and a shirt. For warmth they wrapped themselves in robes of deer or buffalo skin. They decorated their clothing with porcupine quills, elk teeth, shells, and beads. They painted their clothing, especially their robes, with animal pictures and hunting scenes. The men also decorated their bodies with dye from plants and colored clay, and shaved their heads except for a strip in the middle. To this they added deer-tail hairs and feathers.

The life force for the Osage was *Wakonda,* and people could connect to it by having visions. Osage ceremonies were dedicated to making the warriors brave, the hunting successful, and the corn grow. They used corn not only as food, but also in name-giving ceremonies. Infants were rubbed with cornmeal as a protection against evil.

You whose day it is
Make it beautiful.
Get out your rainbow colors,
So it will be beautiful
                    —Nootka

A RAINBOW FOR THE SKY

In the time of long ago Father Sun sent forth his mighty rays upon Mother Earth. The corn in the fields turned brown. The trees curled up their leaves. Animals fled to the mountains, and birds flew away. The water in the rivers dried up, and fish burrowed into muddy bottoms.

"Help us," the people begged the Medicine Man. "Our children cry out in hunger."

"Dance," cried the Medicine Man. "Let the Rain God hear our prayers."

All day long the people danced.

"Boo-oom-oom," pounded the sacred drums.

"Hi . . . iya . . . niho . . . ooo," chanted the people.

All night long the people danced.

"Aha . . . ehe . . . aha . . . ehe," they sang.

"Boo-oom-oom," answered the drums.

High above the earth the Rain God joined the dance. "Oo . . . yi . . . yi," he laughed, his feet bouncing about the clouds.

"The Rain God does not hear us," cried the people.

"Dance faster," said the Medicine Man.

The people shook the earth with their dancing feet.

"Hi . . . iya . . . niho . . . ooo," they wailed, sending clouds of dust swirling across the land.

"Aha . . . ehe . . . aha . . . ehe," chanted the Medicine Man shaking his rattle.

"Boom-oom-oom," echoed the drums.

Deep within Mother Earth a brightly colored snake heard the thunder drums. He listened to the cries of the children. "I must help them," he said, wiggling to the surface of his tunnel.

"I will bring you rain," he said to the Medicine Man.

"How?" laughed the Medicine Man. "Is your magic more powerful than mine?"

"Listen to him," cried the people.

"Pick me up by the tail," said Snake. "Throw me as high as you can."

The Medicine Man seized Snake by the tail. Around and around he twirled. Then up, up, up he threw Snake, high into the sky. When Snake reached the highest clouds, he stretched his body across the sky, from one end of the world to the other.

Back and forth he twisted, up and down he wiggled, scratching his huge body against the clouds. Great chunks of ice broke loose and fell to earth.

It began to rain!

The dry land drank in the cool water.

Still the rain came down.

The corn in the fields reached up straight and trees drank their fill.

Faster and faster came the rain.

The rivers swelled with running waters.

The birds and animals returned to their homes.

Day after day it rained until Mother Earth was washed clean and the thirst of the land was quenched.

Then the great snake rested and the sky cleared.

"Look," cried the people pointing to the sky, "look at Snake. See how his body glows with all the colors of earth and sky."

Great Snake stayed in his heavenly home, never to return to earth again. To this day the people remember him whenever they see a rainbow and they honor him with their dancing feet.

* * *

ABOUT THE SHOSHONE

The Shoshone lived in the Rocky Mountains in what is now Wyoming and some of the most barren desert areas in what is today central and western Idaho, central and northeastern

Nevada, and northwestern Utah. They called their lands *Pia Sokopia,* or "Earth Mother."

Life was hard for the western or desert Shoshone, and survival a constant struggle. Day after day the men roamed the land hunting wild sheep, antelope, squirrels, rabbits, and birds with bows and arrows. The women foraged for seeds, roots, berries, ants, and grasshoppers. Their wanderings depended upon the ripening of the various plants. Some bands stayed in one area long enough to grow corn.

They lived together in small isolated bands of eight to ten persons. In the winter, they built a variety of simple shelters, usually near water and firewood. Some bands made their homes of bark-covered branches, some dug their dwellings out of hillsides.

In the heat of the summer desert, the adults needed little clothing. The men wore loincloths while the women wrapped a kind of apron around their waists. In winter they covered themselves with robes made of rabbit, buffalo, and the fur of other animals.

The eastern Shoshone fared much better as a hunting people where existence was closely tied to the buffalo. On the Plains, they lived in decorated teepees, hunting the buffalo in spring and fall on horseback, fishing, and smoking or drying the meat for the winter. The eastern Shoshone were warriors with strong military societies.

Like most native peoples the Shoshone had no written language and no schools, although the eastern tribe could keep track of large numbers using sticks. The children learned by working alongside adults. They were never spanked or punished. The elders believed such punishment would only break a young person's spirit.

Some Shoshone lived in Idaho near the Snake River. One of them, Sacagawea, was a famous woman who helped shape the course of American history. In 1804 she accompanied Meriwether Lewis and William Clark on their expedition to the Pacific Ocean as a guide and interpreter.

The Shoshone believed in the power of dreams and visions to obtain the help of spirits. To the eastern Shoshone in particular, group ceremonies featuring long dances that lasted for days, like the Sun Dance, helped keep the natural world well. One supreme being was called *Duma Appáh*. Each morning the elders faced the sun in the east and sang a prayer song, believing the rays of the sun carried their words up to *Appáh*.

I shall vanish and be no more,
But the land over which I now roam
Shall remain
And change not.

                                    —Omaha

WHEN THE WORLD ENDS*

SIOUX

It was spoken many moons ago that where the prairies met *Mako Sica*—the Badlands of South Dakota—there was a secret cave.

No one knows where it is.

No one knows how to find it.

No one has ever seen it.

Down through the ages people have searched for it.

They watched the birds soaring high in the sky.

Did the birds know?

They watched the animals crossing the prairies.

◆ ◆ ◆

* This legend was told to Richard Erdoes by Jenny Leading Cloud at White River, South Dakota, and was recorded by him in 1967.

57

Did the animals know?

They followed Bison.

They followed Chipmunk.

They followed Wild Horse.

They followed Eagle.

No one has ever discovered the secret.

Inside the cave lives Old Woman. She has lived there since the beginning of time. Her hair is long and white as snow. Her face is wrinkled as a walnut. Her clothing is made of animal skins trimmed with beads.

No one has ever spoken to her.

No one has ever seen her.

No one knows her name.

All day long Old Woman sits at her loom working on blanket strips made of dyed porcupine quills for a buffalo robe. In and out, in and out, day after day, she weaves the blanket.

Beside her sits Sunka Sapa, her huge black dog. All day long he watches Old Woman, his eyes never moving.

Day after day he sits.

Day after day he watches.

Day after day he waits, licking his paws.

"Soon, Sunka Sapa," says Old Woman patting his head. "Soon we'll eat."

On the far side of the cave burns a fire that keeps them warm. Old Woman started the fire long before the beginning of time. Every day she adds more wood to the flames. Above the fire hangs an earthenware pot. Inside the pot, bubbling and boiling, is *wojapi,* a sweet red berry soup.

As Father Sun walks the western sky, Old Woman pushes herself up from her loom and limps across the cave. She stirs the *wojapi* with a wooden paddle. Because she is so old and so feeble, this takes her a long, long time.

The minute her back is turned, Sunka Sapa jumps to his feet. He tears the porcupine quills from her blanket strip. He tugs and pulls at the strip with his teeth.

"Gr-r-r-r-r-r-r," he tugs.

"Gr-r-r-r-r-r-r," he pulls.

Back across the cave hobbles Old Woman. She sits down at her loom and begins to weave all over again.

The Sioux people say the day she weaves in the last porcupine quill, the day the robe is finished, the world will come to an end.

To this day the robe remains unfinished.

ABOUT THE SIOUX

The people commonly called Sioux consisted of three loose geographic groups, the Dakota (eastern), the Lakota (western), and the Nakota (central). They lived from the woodlands of present-day Wisconsin into Wyoming and Montana, gradually migrating westward across the Plains. They were skilled horsemen and fierce fighters, well known for their bravery. It is the Plains Indian culture of the nineteenth century that is generally portrayed in the movies. Famous Sioux warriors include the Oglala Sioux Crazy Horse and Red Cloud, and the Hunkpapa Sioux medicine man, Sitting Bull.

Also, it was the Sioux in 1876 who were engaged in war against Lieutenant Colonel George Armstrong Custer and the United States Cavalry at the Battle of the Little Bighorn.

Extended families, or clans of Sioux, lived in villages. Their houses were of many different types, depending on the season and the region they lived in. When in search of buffalo and elk, the Sioux lived in tepees which they moved from place to place. They hauled their supplies on a kind of sled pulled by dogs or horses, called a travois.

On the Plains, the men hunted buffalo for food, and used their hides for clothing and shelter. They wore buckskin leggings, shirts, and moccasins made of buffalo or elk hide. The women raised corn, squash, and beans. They wore long elk-skin dresses, leggings, and moccasins as well, and both wrapped themselves in buffalo hides in winter. They decorated their clothing with porcupine quills, elk teeth, beadwork, feathers, fringe, and buffalo hair. The men painted their robes with pictures that told of their ability as hunters and bravery as warriors. Their shields and lances were also painted and trimmed with fur and feathers.

The Sioux honored the all-powerful spirit, *Wakan Tanka-Tunkashila,* the Grandfather Spirit, who created their world and sent them animals for food. They believed that everything had a spirit: animals, plants, wind, rain, sun, water, and thunder. When these spirits were angry they brought sickness and death.

One of their important rites was the vision quest. At age fifteen, a young man set out alone to spend four days and nights without food, water, or shelter. Through fasting and prayer, he hoped to experience a vision, an image, of a special spirit that would give him power and guide him throughout his life. This spirit might be an animal, a bird, or the wind—something that was part of nature.

Among the elaborate rituals of the Sioux were the sacred Sun Dance, the Ghost Dance, the sweat-lodge ceremony, and the smoking of the calumet or peace pipe. They also believed that one day their world would end and a new world would come alive.

SOURCES

BACKGROUND MATERIAL

Johnson, Michael G. *The Native Tribes of North America: A Concise Encyclopedia*. New York: Macmillan Publishing Company, 1994.

Pritzker, Barry M. *A Native American Encyclopedia: History, Culture, and Peoples*. New York: Oxford University Press, 2000.

Waldman, Carl. *Atlas of the North American Indian*. New York: Facts on File, 1985.

The poems and legends in this book may be found in many versions in many sources. The following are some of the ones I have come across in my research.

EPIGRAPH

Cronyn, George W. *American Indian Poetry: An Anthology of Authentic Songs and Chants*. New York: Ballantine Books, 1972, p. 89. (Originally published as *The Path on the Rainbow: An Anthology of Songs and Chants from the Indians of North America*. New York: Boni & Liveright, 1918; Liveright, 1934.)

INTRODUCTION

Poem
Cronyn, p. 58-59.

Fletcher, Alice C. *Indian Games and Dances with Native Songs*. Boston: Birchard, 1915, p. 18.

IN THE BEGINNING

Poem
Astrov, Margot. *American Indian Prose and Poetry*. New York: Capricorn Books, 1962, p. 75. (Originally published as *The Winged Serpent*. New York: John Day, 1946.)

Curtis, Natalie (Natalie Curtis Burlin). *The Indians' Book: Authentic Native American Legends, Lore, and Music.* New York: Bonanza Books, 1987, p. 316. (Originally published New York: Harper & Bros., 1907.)

Densmore, Frances. *Chippewa Music 1.* Bureau of American Ethnology Bulletin no. 45. Washington D.C.: U.S. Government Printing Office, 1910, p. 95.

Legend

Hall, Edwin S., Jr. *The Eskimo Storyteller: Folktales from Noatak, Alaska.* Knoxville: University of Tennessee Press, 1975, pp. 83-85.

Millman, Lawrence. *A Kayak Full of Ghosts: Eskimo Tales.* Santa Barbara, Calif.: Capra Press, 1987, p. 38.

THE-TWO-MEN-WHO-CHANGED-THINGS

Poem

Burlin, Natalie Curtis. *Songs of the Earth.* New York: Harper & Bros., 1935, p. 28.

Cronyn, p. 103.

Legend

Edmonds, Margot and Ella Elizabeth Clark. *Voices of the Wind.* New York: Facts on File, 1989, pp. 13-14.

Swan, James. *The Indians of Cape Flattery at the Entrance to the Strait of Fuca, Washington.* Washington D.C.: Smithsonian Contributions to Knowledge, 1870, pp. 109-111.

THE EARTH DIVER

Poem

Bierhorst, John. *In the Trail of the Wind: American Indian Poems and Ritual Orations.* New York: Farrar, Straus & Giroux, 1971, p. 5.

Radin, Paul. *The Road of Life and Death: A Ritual Drama of the American Indians.* New York: Pantheon Books, 1945, p. 254.

Turner, Frederick W. *North American Indian Reader.* New York: Viking Press, 1974, p. 238.

Legend

Clark, Ella Elizabeth. *Indian Legends of Canada.* Toronto: McClelland & Stewart, 1991, p. 7.

Gill, Sam D. and Irene F. Sullivan. *Dictionary of Native American Mythology.* Santa Barbara, Calif.: Oxford Press, 1992, p. 78.

Hultkrantz, Åke. *The Religions of the American Indians.* Translated by Monica Setterwall. Berkeley: University of California Press, 1980, p. 65.

Mayo, Gretchen Will. *Earthmaker's Tales: North American Stories about Earth Happenings.* New York: Walker, 1989, pp. 3-5.

Miller, Jay. *Earthmaker: Tribal Stories from Native North America.* New York: Perigee, 1992, p. 17.

Wherry, Joseph H. *Indian Masks and Myths of the West.* New York: Funk & Wagnalls, 1969, pp. 193-194.

HOW RAVEN STOLE DAYLIGHT

Poem

Cronyn, p. 295.

Fletcher, Alice C. *The Hako: A Pawnee Ceremony.* Bureau of American Ethnology Annual Report no. 22. Washington D.C.: U.S. Government Printing Office, 1904, p. 5ff.

Legend

Coffin, Tristram P. *Indian Tales of North America.* Philadelphia: American Folklore Society, 1961, pp. 22-24.

Feldman, Susan. *The Storytelling Stone.* New York: Laurel/Dell, 1965, pp. 94-97.

Sheehan, Carol. "The Northwest Coast." In *Native American Myths and Legends,* edited by Colin F. Taylor. New York: Smithmark Publishers, 1994, p. 86.

Wherry, pp. 65-70.

WHY WE HAVE DAY AND NIGHT

Poem

Cronyn, p. 291.

Fletcher, *The Hako: A Pawnee Ceremony;* see under *How Raven Stole Daylight.*

Legend

Thompson, Stith. *Tales of the North American Indians.* Bloomington, Ind.: Indiana University Press, 1966, pp. 39-40. (Originally published 1929.)

Smith, Erminnie A. *Myths of the Iroquois.* Bureau of [American] Ethnology Annual Report no. 2. Washington D.C.: U.S. Government Printing Office, 1883, p. 47ff.

THE STAR CHILDREN

Poem

Cronyn, p. 104.

Russell, Frank. *The Pima Indians.* Tucson: University of Arizona Press, 1975, p. 208. (Originally published as part of Bureau of American Ethnology Annual Report no. 26. Washing-ton D.C.: U.S. Government Printing Office, 1908.)

Legend

Gill and Sullivan, pp. 212-213, 287.

Kavasch, E. Barrie. *Earth Maker's Lodge.* Peterborough, N.H.: Cobblestone Publishing, 1994, p. 40.

PRINCESS GOLDEN BELLS

Poem

Fernández, Adela. *Diccionario ritual de vous Nahuas.* Mexico, D.F.: Panoramo Editorial, 1992, p. 42-C.

Leach, María. *How the People Sang the Mountains Up.* New York: Viking Press, 1969, p. 13.

Legend

Alexander, Hartley Burr. *Mythology of All Races. Vol. X: North American.* Boston: Archaeological Institute of America, Marshall Jones Co., 1916; reprint Cooper Square Publishers, 1964, pp. 51-52.

Markman, Roberta H. and Peter T. Markman. *The Flayed God: The Mesoamerican Mythological Tradition.* San Francisco: Harper San Francisco, 1992, pp. 188-190, 380-381.

ORIGIN OF THE WIND

Poem

Cronyn, p. 68.

Mooney, James. *Songs of the Ghost-Dance Religion,* #6. Bureau of [American] Ethnology Annual Report no. 14. Washington D.C.: U.S. Government Printing Office, 1896, pp. 58-61.

Legend

Edmonds and Clark, pp. 82-84.

Nequatewa, Edmund. *Truth of a Hopi, and Other Clan Stories.* Flagstaff, Ariz.: Northern Arizona Society of Science and Art, 1936, pp. 103-104, 125-126.

SPRING DEFEATS WINTER

Poem

Astrov, p. 121.

Belting, Natalia. *Our Fathers Had Powerful Songs.* New York: Dutton, 1974, unpaged.

Cronyn, p. 347.

Densmore, Frances. *Teton Sioux Music and Culture.* Bureau of American Ethnology Bulletin no. 61. Washington D.C.: U.S. Government Printing Office, 1918, p. 291.

Legend

Bruchac, Joseph. *Native American Stories.* Golden, Colo.: Fulcrum Publishing, 1991, pp. 89-92.

Folktales of the North American Indian. New York: Gramercy Books, 1997, pp. 209-211.

Toye, William. *How Summer Came to Canada.* New York: H.Z. Walck, 1969, unpaged.

THE THEFT OF FIRE

Poem

Cronyn, p. 83.

Matthews, Washington. *The Mountain Chant: A Navajo Ceremony.* Salt Lake City: University of Utah Press, 1997, p. 459. (Originally published 1887.)

Legend

Carden, Gary. "The Southeast." In *Native American Myths and Legends,* edited by Colin F. Taylor. New York: Smithmark Publishers, 1994, p. 86.

Gill and Sullivan, pp. 89-90.

Hulpach, Vladimír. *American Indian Tales and Legends.* London: Paul Hamlyn, 1965, pp. 25-27.

Leach, pp. 49-51.

Mooney, James. *Myths of the Cherokee.* Bureau of American Ethnology Annual Report no. 19. Washington D.C.: U.S. Government Printing Office, 1902, p. 290.

THE FIRST MAN

Poem

Astrov, p. 75.

Belting, unpaged.

Densmore, Frances. *Chippewa Music 1.* Bureau of American Ethnology Bulletin no. 45. Washington D.C.: U.S. Government Printing Office, 1910, p. 95.

Fletcher, Alice C. and Frances LaFlesche. *The Omaha Tribe.* Bureau of American Ethnology Annual Report no. 27. Washington D.C.: U.S. Government Printing Office, 1911, p. 69.

Legend

Emerson, Ellen Russell. *Indian Myths.* Minneapolis: Ross & Haines, 1965, pp. 138-139.

Lyback, Johanna R.M. *Indian Legends of Eastern America.* Chicago: Lyons & Carnahan, 1963, pp. 109-111.

A RAINBOW FOR THE SKY

Poem

Astrov, p. 51-52.

Densmore, Frances. *Nootka and Quileute Music.* Bureau of American Ethnology Bulletin no. 124. Washington D.C.: U.S. Government Printing Office, 1939, pp. 284-285.

Legend

Emerson, pp. 51-52.

Hulpach, pp. 40-41.

Wherry, p. 102.

WHEN THE WORLD ENDS

Poem

Astrov, p. 133.

Fletcher, Alice C. and Francis LaFlesche. *The Omaha Tribe.* Bureau of American Ethnology Annual Report no. 27. Washington D.C.: U.S. Government Printing Office, 1911, p. 475.

Legend

Erdoes, Richard and Alfonson Ortiz. *American Indian Myths and Legends.* New York: Pantheon Books, 1984, p. 485.

POSTSCRIPT

Martinez, José Luis. *Nezahuacoyotl.* Mexico, D.F.: Secretaría de Educación Pública, 1972, p. 47.

❖❖❖❖❖❖❖❖❖❖❖❖❖❖❖❖❖

Will I leave only this:
Like flowers that wither?
Will nothing last in my name?
Nothing of my fate here on earth?
At least flowers!
At least songs!
At least stories!

—Aztec

❖❖❖❖❖❖❖❖❖❖❖❖❖❖❖❖❖